Hiroshima

The Shadow of the Bomb

RICHARD TAMES

Heinemann
LIBRARY

First published in Great Britain by Heinemann Library
Halley Court, Jordan Hill, Oxford OX2 8EJ
a division of Reed Educational & Professional Publishing Ltd.
Heinemann is a registered trademark of Reed Educational & Professional Publishing Ltd.

OXFORD FLORENCE PRAGUE MADRID ATHENS MELBOURNE AUCKLAND
KUALA LUMPUR SINGAPORE TOKYO IBADAN NAIROBI KAMPALA JOHANNESBURG
GABORONE PORTSMOUTH NH (USA) CHICAGO MEXICO CITY SAO PAOLO

Designed by Jim Evoy
Illustrations by Jeff Edwards, Oxford Illustrators
Printed in Hong Kong

02 01 00 99
10 9 8 7 6 5 4 3 2

ISBN 0 431 06882 8

British Library Cataloguing in Publication Data
Tames, Richard, 1946–
Hiroshima: the shadow of the bomb. - (Turning points in history)
1. World War, 1939-1945 - Campaigns - Japan - Hiroshima-shi - Juvenile literature
2. Atomic bomb - Japan - Hiroshima-shi - Juvenile literature
3. World War, 1939-1945 - Aerial operations, American - Juvenile literature
4. Hiroshima-shi, Japan - History - Bombardment, 1945 - Juvenile literature
I. Title
942.5'425

Acknowledgements
Corbis-Bettmann/UPI, pp.4, 14, 15, 16, 25, 27; Honeywell, Chris, p.7;
Popperfoto, pp.6, 12, 18, 22, 23, 26, 29; Tames, Richard, pp.8, 20, 21, 28; TRH Pictures, pp.11, 19;

Cover photograph: PA News

Our thanks to Jane Shuter for her help in the preparation of this book.

Every effort has been made to contact copyright holders of any material reproduced in this book. Any
omissions will be rectified in subsequent printings if notice is given to the Publisher.

Some words are shown in bold, **like this**. You can find out what they mean
by looking in the glossary.

Contents

What happened at Hiroshima? 4

How the atom bomb changed the world 6

The background: how Japan became a threat 8

Crisis and conquest 10

Origins of the atom bomb 12

The (almost) best kept secret of the war 14

No alternative? 16

Why did Japan surrender? 18

Occupation and reconstruction 20

A long time dying 22

Balance of fear 24

Atoms for peace 26

Price of progress 28

Time-line 30

Glossary 31

Index 32

What happened at Hiroshima?

An unsuspecting city

6 August, 1945 was a fine summer's day. World War II had come to an end in Europe, but still Japanese cities were being heavily bombed. As people tried to work on as normal, little did they realize that for thousands of them life was about to come to a terrifying and violent end. Hiroshima had been selected by the USA as the first atomic bomb target.

Just before 9 am, an American bomber, the *Enola Gay*, appeared over the port of Hiroshima. It was carrying a single atomic bomb weighing over 4500 kg. Although many tests had been done, nobody knew for certain what the effect of dropping an atomic bomb on a major city would be.

Death from the sky

The co-pilot Colonel Paul Tibbets released the bomb and the *Enola Gay* quickly climbed to safety. Less than a minute later the bomb exploded. One eyewitness saw a flash so bright she thought a fire had started in her eyes.

A shadow over the world – the mushroom cloud created by the Hiroshima bomb.

She then realized the skin on her face, hands and arms had peeled off. Although they could not see the devastation through the huge cloud of smoke and dust, one of the *Enola Gay*'s crew cried out, *'My God, what have we done?'* The explosion produced a ground temperature of 3000°C – twice as high as the melting-point of iron. An estimated 50,000 people living within 1 km of the blast burned to death. A wind tore through the city at 800 kph, uprooting trees and flattening buildings.

Survivors staggered around in a state of shock. The dead and dying lay all around. Neighbours and total strangers tried to help each other. But there was chaos everywhere. This city of 245,000 people only had 150 doctors. Of these, 65 were killed outright and most of the rest were wounded. Of 1780 nurses, 1654 were dead or too injured to work. At the city's biggest hospital only one doctor out of thirty was uninjured and only five more were able to work. The nursing staff of over 200 was down to ten. 10,000 wounded poured in desperately seeking help.

The final toll

No one knows exactly how many died in Hiroshima on 6 August, 1945. Official figures estimated 100,000. As the months went by the figure rose steadily. **Radiation** sickness was taking its toll. By the end of 1945, the estimate was 140,000.

Hiroshima was a medium-sized port and industrial centre backed by a ring of mountains which enclosed the force of the blast.

JAPAN

Tokyo

Hiroshima

DEATH MARCH

On 7 August, 1945, the day after the bomb was dropped, a Japanese doctor wrote in his diary: *'Hundreds of injured people trying to escape passed our house. Their hands and faces were burned and swollen; great sheets of skin had peeled away like rags on a scarecrow. By this morning there were so many of them lying on both sides of the road it was impossible to pass without stepping on them.'*

How the atom bomb changed the world

The first successful atom bomb test had taken place in July 1945. Robert J Oppenheimer, whose team of scientists made the bomb, said afterwards 'We knew the world would not be the same.' Other people agreed.

On 2 September, 1945, less than a month after atom bombs were dropped on Japan, Douglas MacArthur, an American General, warned that a future war could destroy the entire human race. The terrifying power of atomic weapons made military leaders realize that any country thinking about using one might easily bring disaster on itself as well as its enemy. American General Omar Bradley concluded that *'The way to win an atomic war is to make certain it never starts.'*

Devastated Hiroshima

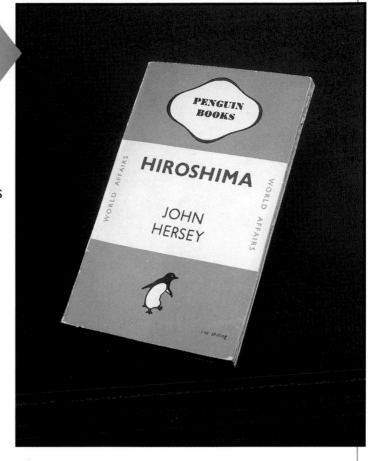

John Hersey's book, *Hiroshima*

Telling the world

In May 1946, the *New Yorker* magazine sent journalist John Hersey to Japan to find survivors of the attack on Hiroshima. He interviewed two doctors, two priests and two women and wrote about what they had suffered and seen. The *New Yorker*'s editor was shocked by Hersey's 30,000 word report. He believed that most people still did not understand how terrible the effects of an atom bomb were.

THE VALUE OF FEAR

In November 1945, Albert Einstein, the world's most famous scientist, wrote:
'I do not believe that civilization will be wiped out in a war fought with the atomic bomb. Perhaps two thirds of the people of the earth might be killed, but enough men capable of thinking, and enough books, would be left to start again, and civilization could be restored. Since I do not foresee that atomic energy is to be a great **boon** *for a long time, I have to say that for the present it is a menace. Perhaps it is as well that it should be. It may* **intimidate** *the human race into bringing order into its international affairs, which, without the pressure of fear, it would not do.'*

He published Hersey's complete account, using one whole issue of the magazine. He thought this would have more impact than spreading it over several weekly issues. He was right. It sold out within hours. Fifty American newspapers reprinted it. It was broadcast on radio in both America and Britain. America's Book of the Month Club published it as a special 'Extra'. In Britain, Penguin Books published 250,000 paperback copies of it.

The background: how Japan became a threat

Opening up the closed country

In 1639, after many years of civil war, Japan cut off trade with other countries, fearing outsiders might cause yet more problems. In 1853, a modern American fleet demanded the right to trade. Japan had fallen far behind in technology and was forced to agree. This humiliation caused years of crisis and confusion, but by 1873 a new government was in power and was determined to make Japan strong by adopting western-style technology. It used foreign experts and imports to rapidly modernize the armed forces, build railways and set up cotton-mills and steel-works. Western-style banks, schools, coinage, weights and measures, newspapers and postal services were introduced.

Japan's modernized army in action.

Empire building

Japan's leaders compared their country to Britain, a small off-shore island. By conquering a huge overseas empire, Britain had become the most powerful country in the world. Japan wanted to do the same. In 1894, Japan and China fought for control over their neighbour, Korea.

This map shows the growth of the Japanese overseas empire.

MANCHURIA
(Japanese occupation 1931–2)

MANCHUKUO
(1934 Empire under Japanese protection)

KOREA

JAPAN

•Tokyo

•Hiroshima

Nagasaki

•Shanghai

CHINA

FORMOSA

| | Japanese Empire before 1928 |
| | Occupied by Japan 1928–36 |

Despite its huge population, China was easily defeated by Japan's more modern armed forces. Japan not only took control of Korea, but also took the Chinese island of Taiwan as the first **colony** of its overseas empire. In 1904–5, Japan fought Russia for control of Korea, and won. In 1910, Korea became part of the Japanese Empire. These successes made Japan's military leaders a powerful influence in government.

TOKYO TRANSFORMED

American teacher W E Griffis was shocked by how poor Japan was when he arrived in rural Echizen in 1870. Within a year he'd been transferred to the capital and was amazed by how it had changed in such a short time:
'Tokyo is so modernized that I scarcely recognize it. There are no beggars on the streets. The age of pantaloons (trousers) has come. Carriages are numerous. The soldiers are all in uniform, as are the police. New bridges span the canals. Gold and silver coins are being used as money in circulation ...'

Problems at home

Despite dramatic progress in building modern industries, Japan still had many problems. Rapid population growth kept many people in poverty. In 1923, a massive earthquake destroyed the capital, Tokyo, and the port of Yokohama, killing 100,000 people and destroying or damaging 3,000,000 homes. America gave millions of dollars to help Japan recover, but in 1924 banned **immigration** by Japanese people. Many Japanese took this ban as a racist insult.

Crisis and conquest

A greater Japan

During the 1920s, **extremists** became more active in politics and in the Japanese army. They argued that the best way for Japan to become rich and respected, was to make its empire even bigger. This would provide Japanese industry with the raw materials it needed, such as coal, iron, rubber and oil, and poor people could leave Japan and start new lives overseas.

Bullying China

Japanese businesses built railways and mined for minerals in Manchuria, a huge, underpopulated part of northern China. The weak Chinese government even allowed Japanese troops to guard the mines and railways. But between 1929 and 1931, world trade collapsed and millions of people lost their jobs. 3,000,000 were out of work in Japan. The country's leaders desperately wanted to expand. So, in 1931, the Japanese army faked a Chinese attack on a Manchurian railway, then used this as an excuse to take over the whole area. In 1937, Japanese generals invaded the rest of China and in 1940, Japan took over French **colonies** in south-east Asia.

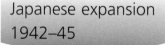

Japanese expansion 1942–45

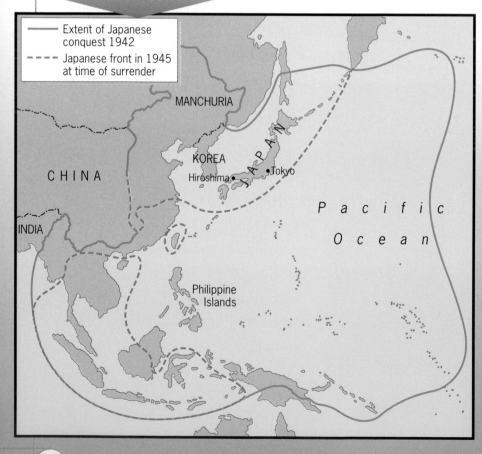

Extent of Japanese conquest 1942

Japanese front in 1945 at time of surrender

MANCHURIA

KOREA

Hiroshima• •Tokyo

CHINA

JAPAN

INDIA

P a c i f i c

O c e a n

Philippine Islands

Success in the Pacific

America protested at Japan's actions. The American government tried to stop Japan's expansion by refusing to sell its government oil or steel. But Japan still refused to withdraw from its conquests. Believing war with America was unavoidable, in December 1941, the Japanese airforce made a devastating surprise attack on the US Navy base at Pearl Harbor, Hawaii. For the next six months Japanese forces triumphed everywhere. They took the Philippines from America, and Hong Kong and Singapore from Britain.

The attack on Pearl Harbor.

The tide turns

Then, in June 1942, the Japanese lost four aircraft-carriers in a decisive naval battle off Midway Island in the Pacific. The weakened Japanese navy was now unable to stop American forces from recapturing Pacific islands. By 1944, the US could send bombers against Japan. But bombing Japan was one thing; invading Japan was quite another. American forces were about to discover just how fiercely the Japanese would defend their territory.

The price of victory

In April 1945, US forces landed on the off-shore Japanese island of Okinawa. It took three months to conquer it. 110,000 of its 120,000 Japanese defenders died in the fighting. 34 US ships were sunk, 368 damaged, 12,500 men killed and 36,600 wounded. If that was the price to be paid for taking one island of 500 square miles what would it cost to take Japan itself?

The (almost) best kept secret of the war

The Manhattan Project

The Manhattan Project was the top-secret effort to build an atomic bomb. It took its code name from the district of New York where the early research was done. The scientists working in the USA included Americans, Britons, Canadians and European **refugees**. Their work needed large workshops and laboratories and much special technical equipment. Project centres were also built at remote sites in Tennessee, Washington and New Mexico. The costs involved ran to $2,000,000,000.

The first test

The first atomic bomb was successfully exploded at Alamagordo air base, New Mexico on 16 July, 1945. Placed on a steel tower it created an explosion equal to 20,000 tonnes of TNT. The heat was so intense that the tower simply disappeared and the desert sand 700 metres around its site was turned to glass.

Top secret?...

Only the most important **Allied** leaders and generals knew that there was a bomb project.

'Little Boy' – the bomb that wiped out a city.

Not quite

Thanks to German-born Klaus Fuchs, who worked on the Manhattan Project but was also a Soviet agent, Stalin, leader of the **USSR**, also knew about the bomb project.

In fact the war in Europe had ended when the first bomb was exploded. But thousands of men were being transported to the Far East, to prepare for the invasion of Japan. The war there was expected to last at least another year and a half. Even Allied commanders in the area had no idea that it would be over within a month.

Japanese efforts to make an atomic bomb had been held back by shortages of staff and money. The scientists themselves did not think the matter urgent because they believed that, although in theory it was possible to make one, in practice, not even the USA would be able to do so in the foreseeable future. German scientists were also working on a bomb project but had to give up when Norwegian resistance fighters **sabotaged** the underground factory making material they needed.

Robert J. Oppenheimer and General Groves examine the remains of the steel tower which had supported the first A-bomb successfully exploded

A JAPANESE BOMB?

In 1949, researcher Chitoshi Yanaga admitted that, when news about Hiroshima leaked through to them *'Japanese scientists knew immediately that it was the atomic bomb, for they too had been working on it for years.'* In the two weeks between Japan's surrender and the arrival of US occupation forces much of the evidence of this work was deliberately destroyed.

Why did Japan surrender?

Soldiering on

On 7 August, 1945, the day after Hiroshima's destruction, Japanese radio simply announced that it had been attacked with 'a new kind of bomb'. No contact was made with the **Allies**. Instead Japan, which was not at war with the **USSR**, tried to persuade the Russians to become a go-between to start **negotiations** for peace. On 8 August, the Japanese ambassador met the Soviet Foreign Minister – who told him the USSR was declaring war on Japan. Two hours later **Soviet** troops invaded Manchuria.

The second bomb

On 9 August, another A-bomb was dropped, on the port of Nagasaki. Although it was much more powerful than the Hiroshima bomb, it did less damage because the city's hilly site lessened the force of the blast. Even so about 50,000 people died and a third of all buildings were completely destroyed.

Some Japanese generals still wanted to fight on. Japan is very mountainous, an ideal country for **guerrilla** fighting. Resistance like the defence of Okinawa could cost an invader perhaps a million casualties. Japanese **extremists** were prepared to fight on, with civilians armed with bamboo spears prepared to suffer high casualties in order to defend Japan and force a negotiated peace.

Nagasaki was a major ship-building centre.

The Japanese government was completely divided over what to do. In the end the Emperor broke the deadlock and Japan surrendered on 14 August, 1945.

Were the bombs decisive?

It seemed obvious to many people that the atom bombs hastened the end of the war and so saved the lives an invasion would have cost. But the war might have been ended in other ways. Ordinary bombing could have continued, without a land invasion, until Japan gave in. Some Japanese leaders feared their rice fields would be fire-bombed just before harvest – the country could have been starved out.

Living in the ashes – a Japanese family camp out in the ruins of their Nagasaki home.

Were the USSR's actions decisive?

Some people argue that the USSR's declaration of war against Japan speeded up Japan's surrender. They suggest that Japanese leaders feared an invasion by both the USSR and the US-led Allies. They thought Japan would be permanently divided between the invaders. This did happen in Germany. Worse still, if the USSR took over all of Japan, it would abolish the Emperor and establish a **communist** government. As the Japanese wanted to keep their old ways of ruling, surrendering quickly to the USA, which was likely to be a less brutal occupier, seemed the best option.

Time-line

1639	Japan cuts off foreign trade
1853	USA forces Japan to re-open foreign trade
1894	Japan defeats China and takes over Taiwan
1905	Japan defeats Russia
1910	Japan takes over Korea
1923	Earthquake destroys Tokyo and Yokohama
1924	USA bans immigration by Japanese
1929	World trade collapses
1931	Japan takes over Manchuria
1937	Japan attempts to conquer all of China
1941	December 7th – Japan attacks US naval base at Pearl Harbor, Hawaii
1942	June – Japanese navy defeated at Battle of Midway
1944	US begins bombing of Japan
1945	March – US bombers devastate Tokyo
	April – US forces invade Okinawa
	May – Germany surrenders
	July 16 – First successful atom bomb test at Alamagordo air base, New Mexico
	August 6 – Atom bomb dropped on Hiroshima
	August 8 – USSR declares war on Japan
	August 9 – Atom bomb dropped on Nagasaki
	August 14 – Japan surrenders
	August 28 – US troops land in Japan
1949	North Atlantic **Treaty** Organization founded
1951	Peace treaty signed between Japan and USA
1952	USA tests first Hydrogen bomb
1954	USS *Nautilus* launched
1955	USSR found the Warsaw pact
1964	Olympic games held in Tokyo
1974	India tests an atomic bomb
1979	Nuclear radiation leak at Three Mile Island, Pennsylvania
1986	Nuclear reactor meltdown at Chernobyl, Ukraine
1991	Break-up of USSR ends Cold War

Glossary

Allies	friendly nations
blockade	use ships to prevent goods entering a country
boon	something that is useful
cataract	a clouding of the lens of the eye, causing loss of sight
cobalt	silver-white metal which can be made radioactive to cure some kinds of cancer
colony	land in one place ruled by a foreign government in another place
communism	system of government based on the idea that a single ruling political party can run a country for all its people's benefit better than if they are left to make their own decisions and keep their own private homes, land and businesses
democracy	system of government based on the idea that all citizens have equal rights to speak on political matters and take part freely in choosing and changing their leaders
disarmament	giving up weapons
dismantle	take to pieces
evacuated	taken to safety
extremist	someone with such strong views that they are not prepared to give way
fanatic	extremist who is prepared to use violence
guerrilla	irregular fighter, not part of a recognised army
immigration	people going to live in one country from another country
intimidate	frighten
kilowatts	thousand watts; a watt is the basic unit for measuring electricity
leukemia	a cancer of the blood
negotiations	settle a problem or dispute by talking; usually both sides agree to give up part of their demands
occupation	rule by a foreign army
radiation	energy given off by atomic material
refugees	people forced to leave their home or country
sabotage	deliberate damage to stop something working properly
Soviet	belonging to the Soviet Union (USSR)
trade union	organization to protect and improve the rights and interests of workers
treaty	official agreement between different countries
USSR	Union of Soviet Socialist Republics; an empire in which communist Russia controlled neighbouring countries from 1917 to 1991

Index

Alamagordo, New Mexico 14
Aldermaston march 25
America 6, 7, 8, 9, 11, 16, 17, 20, 22, 24-5, 26, 27, 29
atomic bomb (A-bomb) 4-5, 12-15, 18, 19
atomic power stations 26, 28, 29
atomic-powered submarines 26, 29
atomic warfare 6, 7, 13, 28
atoms 12

bombing raids 4-5, 16, 19
Bradley, General Omar 6
Brazil 29
Britain 7, 8, 11, 16, 25, 26, 29
burn victims 5, 22

Campaign for Nuclear Disarmament (CND) 25
cancer treatment 26
chain reaction 12, 13
Chernobyl 27
China 8, 9, 10, 29
cobalt 26
Cold War 24-5
colonies 9, 10
Cuban crisis 24-5
Czech Republic 25

death toll 5
democratic government 20
dismantling weapons 29
doctors and nurses 5
Dower, John 21

earthquake 9
Einstein, Albert 7, 12, 13
empire building 8-9, 10
Enola Gay 4, 5

first atomic bomb test 14
France 29
Fuchs, Klaus 15

Germany 15, 16, 17, 19, 24
Greenham Common 25
ground temperature 5

Groves, General 15
guerilla warfare 18

Hersey, John 7
hibakusha 22-3
Hirohito, Emperor 19, 20
Hiroshima 4-5, 7, 18, 23, 29
Hiroshima Dome 23
Hong Kong 11
hospitals 5
'hot line' 25
Hungary 25
hydrogen bomb (H-bomb) 24

immigration 9
India 29
industrial growth 10, 21, 27
international co-operation 26
invasion of Japan 11, 15, 16
Iraq 29
Israel 29

Japan 6-11, 15, 16, 17, 18-23, 27
Japanese Empire 9, 10

Kennedy, President John 24
Khrushchev, Nikita 25
Korea 8, 9

Leahy, Admiral 17
'Little Boy' 14

MacArthur, General Douglas 6, 20
Manchuria 10, 18
Manhattan Project 14, 15
maps
    Cuban crisis 24
    Japanese Empire 9, 10
memorial services 23
Midway Island 11
military alliances 24
modernization of Japan 8, 9

Nagasaki 18, 19, 23
Nautilus 26
Neutron bombs 28
New Yorker 7
North Atlantic Treaty Organization (NATO) 24, 25
nuclear accidents 27, 28

nuclear waste 28, 29

occupation of Japan 20
Okinawa 11, 18
Oppenheimer, Robert J 6, 15
origins of the atomic bomb 12-14

Pakistan 29
peace negotiations 18
Peace Park 23
peaceful uses of atomic power 26-7, 28, 29
Pearl Harbor 11
Philippines 11
Poland 25
pollution 28, 29
population growth 9
Potsdam peace conference 16
protest movements 25

radiation sickness 5, 22
radioactive fallout 27
reconstruction of Japan 20-1
Roosevelt, President Franklin D 13

Sakomizu, Hisatune 17
Singapore 11
South Africa 29
Stalin, Joseph 15
surrender of Japan 19
survivors 5, 22-3
Szilard, Leo 13, 17

Taiwan 9
terrorism 29
test bans 25
Three Mile Island 27
Tibbets, Colonel Paul 4
Tokyo 9, 16
Trident nuclear missiles 28
Truman, President 17

uranium 13
USSR 9, 16, 17, 18, 19, 24-5, 26, 27, 29

Warsaw Pact 24, 25
World War II 4, 15, 16

Yokohama 9